ENCORES FOR CHOIRS 1

24 Show-stopping Concert Pieces

Compiled by Peter Gritton

MUSIC DEPARTMENT

OXFORD
UNIVERSITY PRESS

OXFORD
UNIVERSITY PRESS

Great Clarendon Street, Oxford OX2 6DP, England
198 Madison Avenue, New York, NY10016, USA

Oxford University Press is a department of the University of Oxford.
It furthers the University's aim of excellence in research, scholarship,
and education by publishing worldwide

Oxford is a registered trade mark of Oxford University Press
in the UK and in certain other countries

19

ISBN 978-0-19-343630-5

Music origination by Figaro

Printed in Great Britain on acid-free paper by
Caligraving Ltd., Thetford, Norfolk

PREFACE

Encores for Choirs 1 contains 24 pieces in an amazing variety of styles and moods, from which the SATB choir can choose some great 'encore' material or pieces that would suit the lighter end of a concert programme. Humorous, comforting, dazzling, quirky, sentimental, classic, spiritual . . . it's all here!

On the whole, the pieces in *Encores for Choirs 1* are short and of lighter character, with the exception of two of the most popular longer choral encores, 'Geographical Fugue' and 'Italian Salad', without which no volume of this sort would be complete. **Geographical Fugue** by Ernst Toch (1887–1964) was written as the last movement of a suite called *Gesprochene Musik* ('Spoken Music'), first performed at the Berlin Festival of Contemporary Music in 1930. Perhaps the inclusion of so many place names west of the Atlantic was a premonition of Toch's ultimate home, the United States, where he settled six years later. **Italian Salad** by Richard Genée (1823–95) was written originally for male voices and mocks the operatic style of the early nineteenth century. The effect is probably just as comical today as a century and a half ago when it was composed.

The Lost Chord by Sir Arthur Sullivan (1842–1900) is a deceptively melodramatic piece composed over the course of one gruelling night as Sullivan sat contemplating the imminent death of his brother Frederick. Towards the end of his own life Sullivan claimed 'I have composed much music . . . but have never written a second "Lost Chord"'. Several arrangements exist, but the one printed here is one I have written specially, in an up-to-date style.

Sir Henry Bishop (1786–1855) was once somewhat exaggeratedly described as 'the English Mozart'. He could certainly write a good tune, however, as proven by his ballad **Home, sweet home**. The melody alone was written in 1816 but became inextricably linked to words written in 1823 by the American poet John Howard Payne. Since then it has become so popular that it is now often mistaken for a folksong. As with 'The Lost Chord', Bob Chilcott's version of 'Home, sweet home' lifts the harmony out of its nineteenth-century bathos into a more up-to-the-minute style.

Pieces containing silly animal noises have always amused people of all ages. George Mitchell, the famous American arranger, has turned the old nursery rhyme **Old McDonald had a farm** into a classic, with his impeccable sense of timing and fun. Also on the theme of animals, **The Goslings** is a witty but poignant tale of love with a fateful twist, set to music by Sir Frederick Bridge, Organist of Westminster Abbey from

1882 to 1918. Humorous tales personified by animals were abundant in the late nineteenth century and obviously titillated Victorian senses, especially when slightly macabre—as in this poem by Fred Weatherley.

What shall we do with the drunken sailor? is perhaps the most popular sea shanty of all time. Shanties were originally working songs sung by sailors to lift their spirits and put rhythm and impetus into their duties. Jonathan Willcocks's arrangement on the other hand teases us with uneven rhythms and humorous vocal effects to create a breath-taking arrangement, ideal as a finale. The other song of the sea in this volume is John Whitworth's well-known version of **The Mermaid**. It tells of a romantic liaison between a drowned sailor and a mermaid—an age-old myth that helped dispel a mariner's fears of dying at sea.

Charles Villiers Stanford (1852–1924) was possibly the greatest composer to have been born in Ireland. Although he spent only his childhood there, he honoured his roots with an *Irish Symphony*, a series of *Irish Rhapsodies*, and many folksong arrangements. Stanford's source for **Quick! We have but a second** was Thomas Moore's famous *Irish Melodies*, an early nineteenth-century folk collection.

John Gardner (b. 1917) is an English composer renowned for his skill at integrating various idioms, like jazz and ethnic, into his own direct musical style. **Rejection**, written for the Cork Festival of 1975, is an unusual and original piece, clearly doused in a rhythmic Irish folk tradition. Another piece inspired by Irish folk music is Bob Chilcott's **Irish Blessing**. Chilcott was for many years a chief arranger for the King's Singers, and his talents are certainly on show in his beautiful version of the classic **Londonderry Air**. (It is interesting to note that the words, which we all assume to be rooted in an anonymous Irish folklorish past, are actually by the same poet as Bridge's 'The Goslings'—Fred Weatherley.)

Steal away is one of the oldest and best-loved spirituals. In the eighteenth and nineteenth centuries a number of American writers commented on a type of music popular among the slaves of the Deep South. This music was originally sung in unison as the slaves went about their labours, but from the 1860s, and especially after the abolition of slavery, printed collections of harmonized spirituals became readily available. The popularity of this genre was further encouraged by The Jubilee Singers, an internationally acclaimed Afro-American vocal ensemble who toured Europe and the USA during the 1870s. The contrast between 'Steal away' and **Sourwood mountain**, a carefree American fiddle-song from Tennessee, couldn't be greater. John Rutter's skilful arrangement captures the style and its era perfectly with open-string and pizzicato effects and an infectious gaiety.

Nonsense songs have long been popular types of folksong in the pubs and clubs of England and were often written as lengthy ballads about eccentric individuals, such as Michael Finnigin. **Two for the price of one** by Andrew Carter is a clever fusion of two such British folksongs—'There was an old man' and 'This old man'—and demonstrates encore writing at its most playful. In contrast, the character who finds herself centre-stage in Guy Turner's delightful love-song **Tequila Samba** is neither eccentric nor larger than life, but the unwitting object of the author's admiration as she quaffs the tequilas!

Grayston Ives, at one time a member of the King's Singers, thrills us with his original and ingenious composition **Name that tune**, in which at least a dozen classical melodies weave seamlessly in and out of each other to dazzling effect.

John Rutter's music is known throughout the world through recordings made by his choir the Cambridge Singers. But it is through his strong association with the King's Singers that **Banquet Fugue, Home is a special kind of feeling**, and **Let's begin again** came to be written. Each was composed for entertainments performed by the King's Singers and the City of London Sinfonia. ('Home is . . . ' comes from *The Wind in the Willows* and 'Let's begin again' from *The Reluctant Dragon*); all are perfect leave-taking pieces. Andrew Carter's arrangement of **Christopher Robin is saying his prayers** falls into the same category in terms of its sentimental charm; this is original pre-Disney Pooh Bear music written by Harold Fraser-Simson (1872–1944). Fraser-Simson was a ship-owner who turned professional musician after the success of his songwriting hobby in the early 1900s—the heyday of the variety theatre and music hall. **I do like to be beside the seaside** and **The Teddy Bears' Picnic**, arranged here by Andrew Carter, are both from this tradition, although the latter would also have gained popularity through recordings and sales of sheet music.

This collection concludes with Iván Eröd's compact and punchy **Viva la musica**, whose message—'Long live music'—just about says it all!

Encores for Choirs 1 contains an equal mix of original compositions and arrangements. Two thirds of the pieces are designed for performance 'a cappella'—although a helpful piano reduction has been included where necessary—whilst the remainder of the pieces are accompanied.

PETER GRITTON

CONTENTS

Acknowledgements

Thanks must go to all those who sent in suggestions and ideas for the shape and content of the anthology. Any items not included were on probably the longest 'shortlist' in the world. I am particularly indebted to the thorough and energetic editorial work of Paul Keene, who moved on into new pastures just before the completion of the project.

Compiler and General Editor

Peter Gritton studied music at Clare College, Cambridge before taking up a post at Christ Church, Oxford as a countertenor Lay Clerk. Peter has sung with a variety of groups including The Sixteen, The Cambridge Singers, Gabrieli Consort, I Fagiolini, and a close harmony group, The Light Blues, with whom he has travelled worldwide. He currently teaches at St Paul's School, London, as well as enjoying a busy schedule composing, arranging, and singing.

Peter has had arrangements commissioned by the King's Singers. His music is published widely, including some arrangements in the close harmony anthology *In the Mood* and two carols, *Away in a manger* (composed on a new tune) and *Run with torches*, all available from Oxford University Press.

1. Banquet Fugue

David Grant

JOHN RUTTER

This piece is from *The Reluctant Dragon*, an Entertainment originally written for the King's Singers and the City of London Sinfonia. Instrumental material (double bass, drums, piano) is available for hire from the publisher. Also available separately, x431 (excl. USA).

© Oxford University Press 1984.

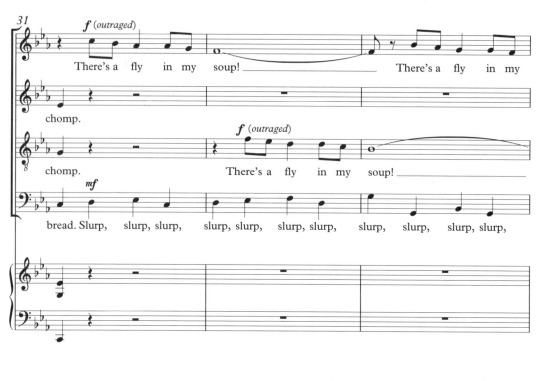

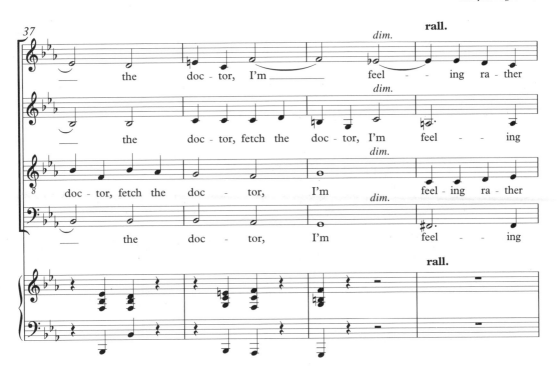

2. Christopher Robin is saying his prayers
(Vespers)

A. A. Milne

H. FRASER-SIMSON
arr. ANDREW CARTER

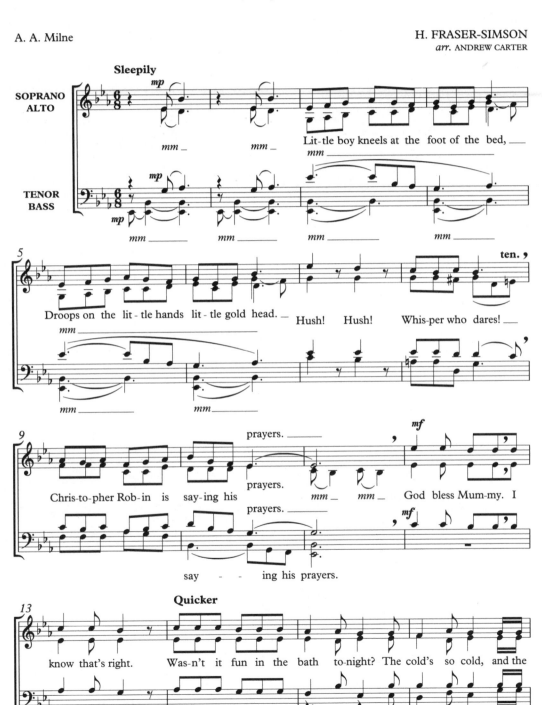

3. Drunken sailor

Traditional shanty
arr. JONATHAN WILLCOCKS

* piano for rehearsal only

morn - ing. What shall we doo doo ____ doo doo doo _ doo doo doo doo
doo doo doo

morn-ing. What shall we do? doo doo doo doo doo _ doo doo doo doo

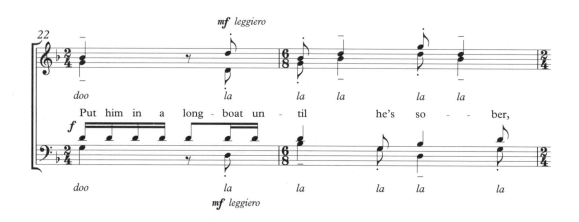

doo la la la la la
Put him in a long - boat un - til he's so - - ber,

doo la la la la la

la la la la la
put him in a long - boat un - til he's so - - ber,

la la la la la la

la la la la
la la la la la la la
put him in a long - boat un - til he's so - - ber

la la la la la la

morn - ing. Hoo - ray! Hoo -
morn - ing. Hoo - ray and up she ris - es, hoo - ray and
morn-ing. Hoo - ray! Hoo - ray! Hoo - ray!
morn-ing. Hoo - ray and up she ris - es, hoo - ray and

ray! Hoo - ray and up she ris - es ear - ly in the
up she ris - es, Hoo - ray! ear - ly in the
Hoo-ray! Hoo - ray and up she ris - es ear - ly in the
up she ris - es, Hoo - ray! ear - ly in the

morn - ing. What shall we *doo doo* _____ *doo doo doo _ doo doo doo doo*

morn-ing. What shall we do?   *Doo doo doo doo doo _ doo doo doo doo*

Pull out the plug and wet him all o - - ver,

doo   la   la   la   la   la

doo   la   la   la   la   la

pull out the plug and wet him all o - - ver,

la   la   la   la   la   la

la   la   la   la   la   la

pull out the plug and wet him all o - - ver

la   la   la   la   la   la

la   la   la   la   la   la

morn - ing.   What shall we *doo doo* _____ *doo doo doo* _ *doo doo doo doo*

doo doo

morn-ing. What shall we do?   *doo doo doo doo doo* _ *doo doo doo*

doo   *la*   *la*   *la*   *la*   *la*

Make him walk the plank and then keel - haul him,

la   *la*   *la*   *la*

la   *la*   *la* *la*   *la* *la* *la*

make him walk the plank and then keel - haul him,

la

la   *la* *la la* *la la la* ear - ly in the

make him walk the plank and then keel - haul him

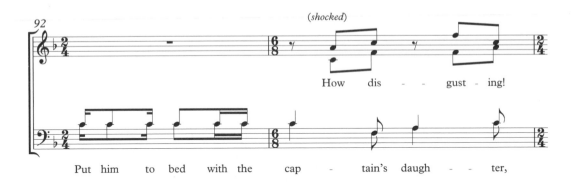

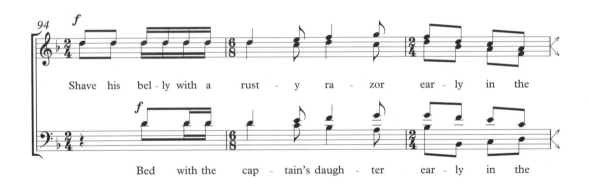

4. Geographical Fugue

for Speaking Chorus

ERNST TOCH

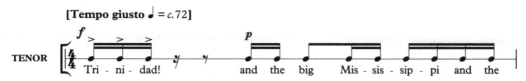

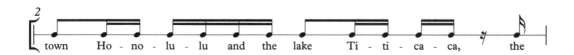

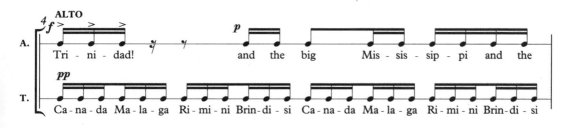

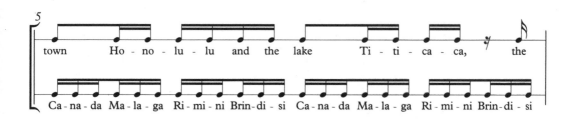

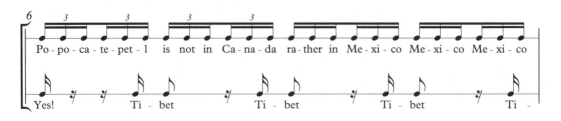

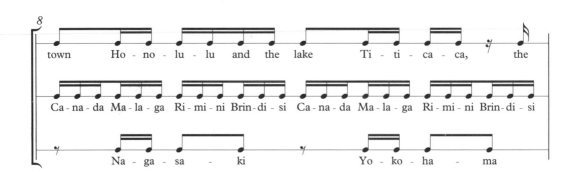

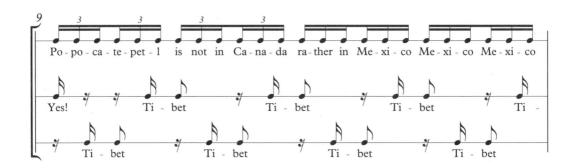

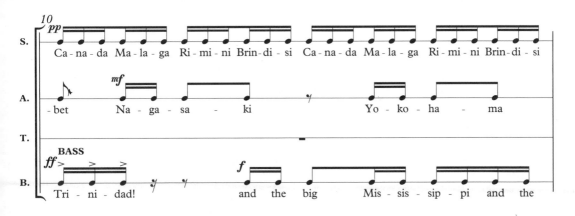

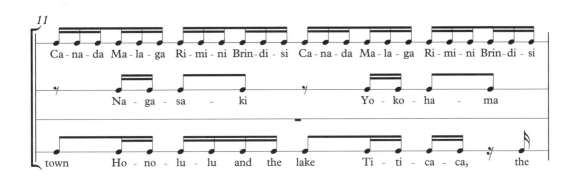

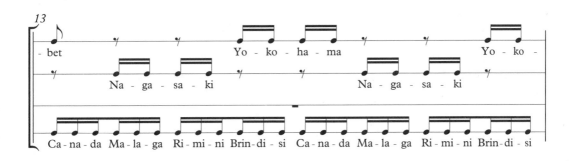

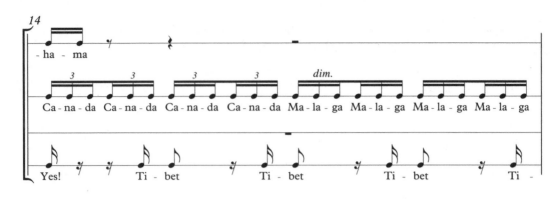

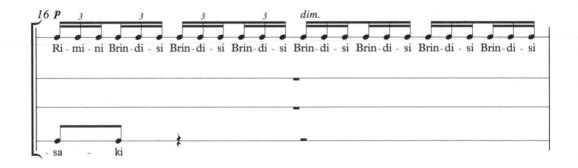

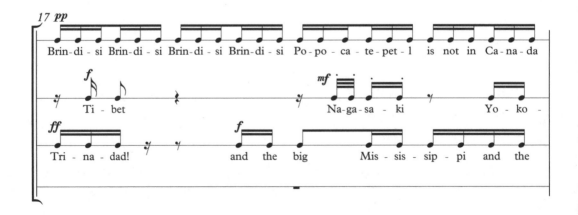

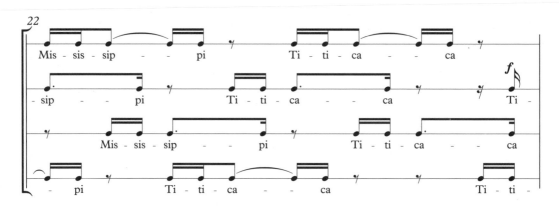

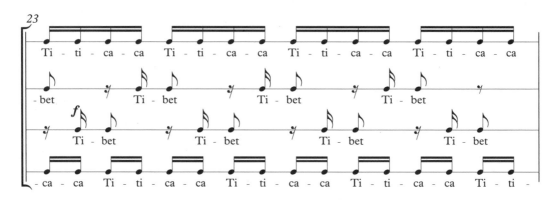

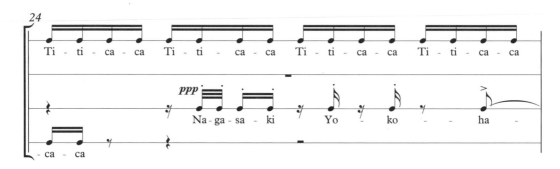

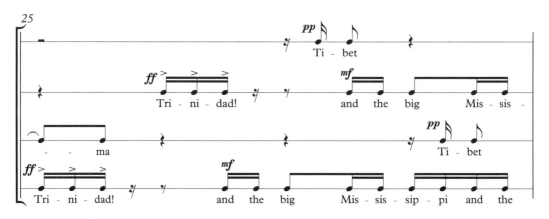

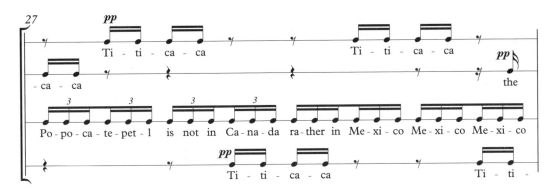

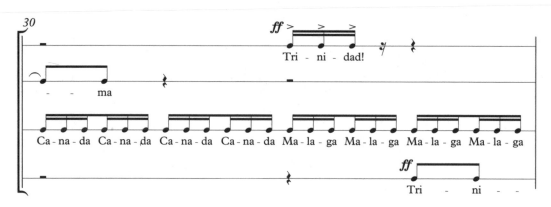

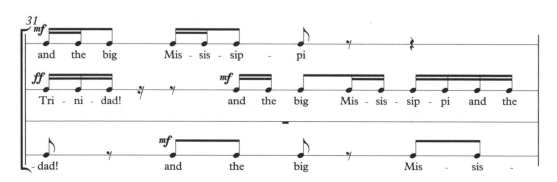

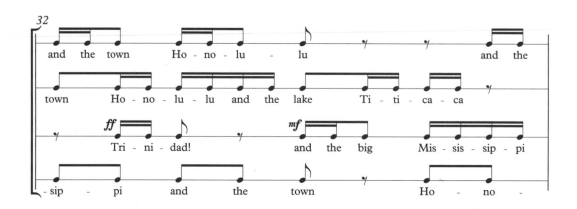

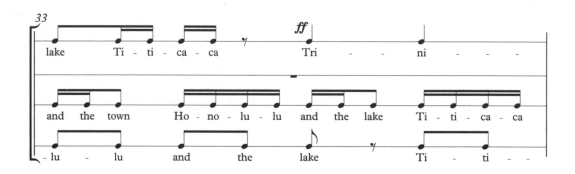

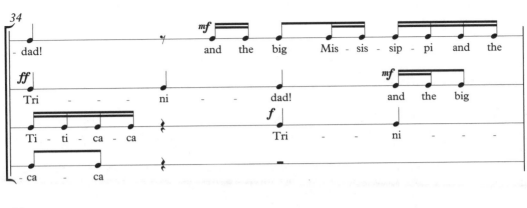

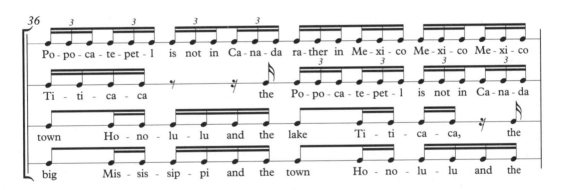

'This piece is the last movement of a suite *Gesprochene Musik* ('Spoken Music') which, from different angles, tries to produce musical effects through speech. The suite was performed and recorded at the Berlin Festival of Contemporary Music in 1930. The record got lost or was destroyed, likewise the music, except the manuscript.' *Ernst Toch*

5. The Goslings

F. E. Weatherley

FREDERICK BRIDGE

Tempo I

Tempo a la marcia

* If preferred, the hummed section may be played instead, with octave reinforcement in the left hand and the first two
notes of the tenor taken up the octave by the right hand.

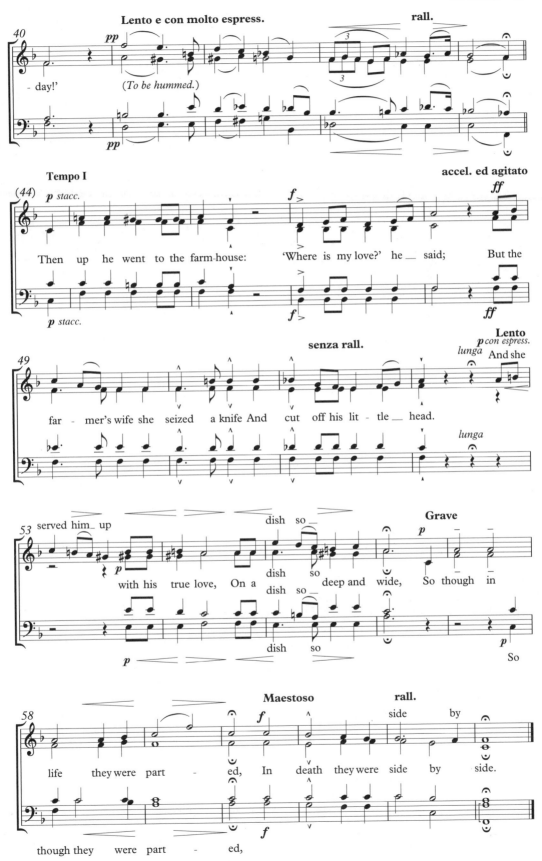

6. Home is a special kind of feeling

David Grant

JOHN RUTTER

This song is the finale from *The Wind in the Willows*, an Entertainment originally written for the King's Singers and the City of London Sinfonia. Orchestral material (flute, oboe, harp, percussion, strings) is available for hire from the publisher. Also available separately, x430 (excl. USA).

7. Home, sweet home

John Howard Payne

HENRY BISHOP
arr. BOB CHILCOTT

8. I do like to be beside the seaside

JOHN A. GLOVER-KIND
arr. ANDREW CARTER

I'd re-side by the side of the sil-ve-ry sea. _____ But
pom   pom   pom   p - p - p - pom   sil - ve-ry   sea,   p - p - p -

when you're just a com-mon or gar - den work - ing lad like me, _____ A
pom   pom   pom   pom   pom   pom   pom   pom

chance* to see the sea _____ is quite a no - vel - ty; _____ I
pom   pom   pom   pom   pom   pom   pom   pom

save up all the mon - ey I can while win - ter's grim and grey, _____ Then
pom   pom   pom   pom   pom   pom   pom   pom

molto rall.

off I run to have some fun where the balm - y breez - es play. Oh! I
pom   pom   pom   pom   pom   pom   pom

* with a northern, short 'a' vowel (likewise 'brass' in bar 49)

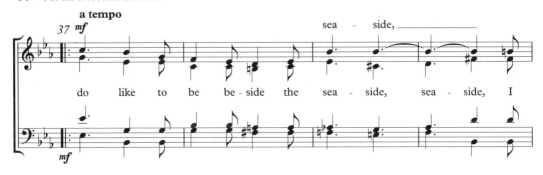

a tempo

37 *mf*

sea - side, ____

do   like   to   be   be - side   the   sea - side,   sea - side,   I

mf

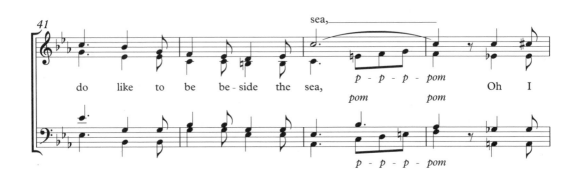

41

sea, ____

do   like   to   be - side   the   sea,   *p - p - p - pom*   Oh   I

pom   *pom*

p - p - p - pom

45

do   like   to   stroll   up - on   the   prom,   prom,   prom   Where   the

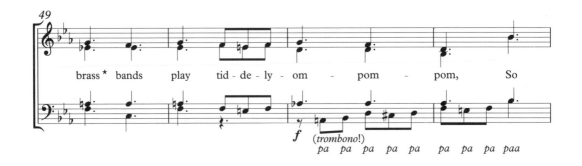

49

brass * bands   play   tid - de - ly - om - pom - pom,   So

f *(trombono!)*

pa   pa   pa   pa   pa   pa   pa   pa   paa

for Grupo Vocal Olisipo

9. Irish Blessing

Traditional

BOB CHILCOTT

And un-til we meet a - gain,

dolce May God hold you, may God hold you ev - er in the

palm of His hand.

May the road rise to meet you, __ may the wind be ev-er at your

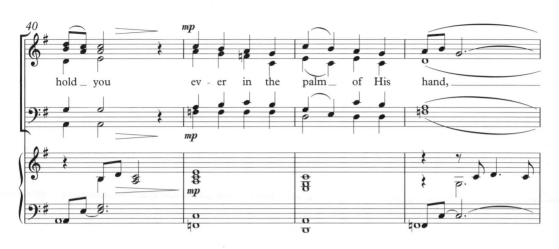

hold _ you   ev - er in the palm _ of His   hand,_____

poco rit.   **A little slower**

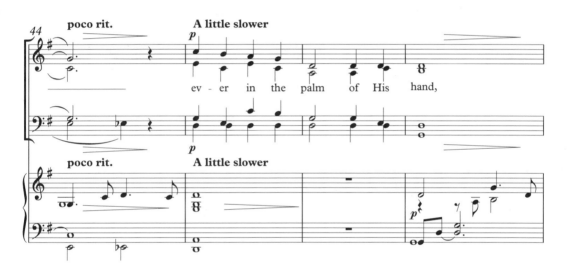

ev - er in the palm of His   hand,

poco rit.   **A little slower**

the palm   of His hand.

rit. e dim.

10. Italian Salad

A musical jest in the form of the Finale to an Italian Opera

RICHARD GENÉE
arr. C. E. ROWLEY

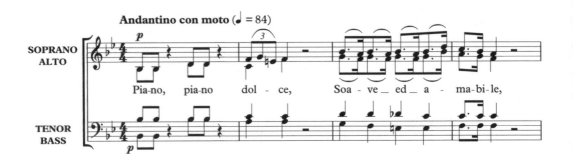

Glossary of Pronunciation. The effect of this piece will be enhanced by using Italian pronunciation:
a=ah. e=é (as in *get*). *i=ee* (but short as in *sit* for the second syllable of *pianissimo, fortissimo, bravissimo*).
o - nearer *got* than *goat*. *u=oo* (short in *wrumm, tutti, un;* all others long). Every vowel and every *r* must be clearly enunciated. *ce* and *ci* - *c* as *ch* in chair. *co* and *ca* - *c* as *k*. *ge, gi* and *ggi* - as *j*. *gh* - hard *g*. *gn* = *ny*. *quà* = *kwah*.
sch = *sh* (*sic*). *z* and *zz* = *ts*.

(Optional cut to p.62, b.88)

-ce - re!   a pi-a - ce - re!   fer - ma - ta, fer - ma - - - ta!

col-la par-te!   col-la par-te!   col - la par-te!

Larghetto (♩ = 76)

Len - to con es - pres - sio - ne!   Lar - ghet - - to, sos-te-nu-to, ri-te-nu-to,

Wrumm! *

Es - pres-si - vo ben mar - ca - to,   Con do-

sos-te-nu-to,   ri-te-nu-to,   sos-te-nu-to,   ri-te-nu-to,   sos-te-nu-to,   ri-te-nu-to,

Wrumm!   Wrumm!   Wrumm!   Wrumm!   Wrumm!   Wrumm!

* pronounced 'Vroom!'

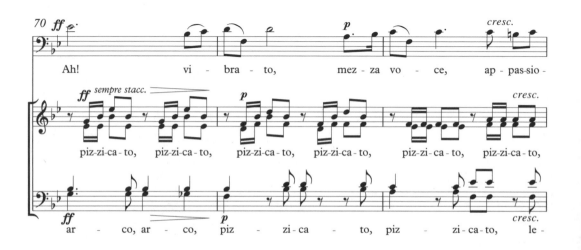

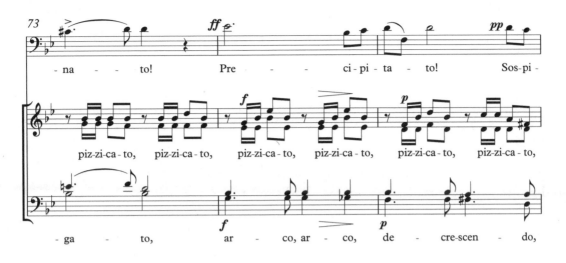

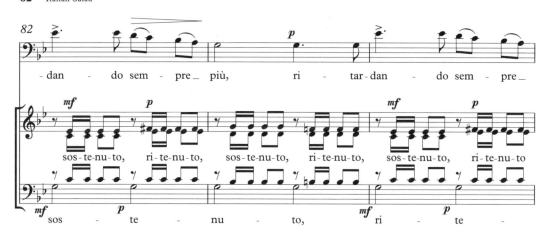

-dan - do sem - pre _ più,   ri - tar-dan - do sem - pre _

sos - te-nu - to,   ri - te-nu - to,   sos - te-nu - to,   ri - te-nu - to,   sos - te-nu - to,   ri - te-nu - to

sos - te - nu - to,   ri - te -

più.

sos-te-nu - to,   ri - te-nu - to,   ri - te - nu - to!

-nu - to,   sos- te-nu - to,   ri - te-nu - to,   ri - te-nu - to!

Allegro

Suo - na la trom-ba,

Tra ta ta ta ta ta ta ta!   Tra ta ta ta ta ta ta ta!

94

A la ven-det-ta! Trom-bon - i, Tim-pan - i, Fa - got - ti! Con-tra-

98

Ve-ni-te tut - ti   a la ven-det - ta,   a la ven-

- bas - si, Vi-o-li - ni, Clar-in - et - ti!   Si!   Si!

(Optional cut to p.65, b.135)

102

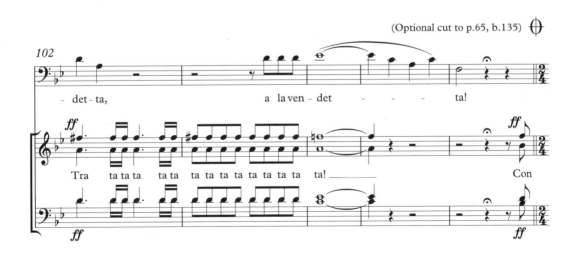

- det - ta,   a la ven - det - - - ta!

Tra ta ta ta   ta ta   ta ta ta ta ta ta ta   ta!   Con

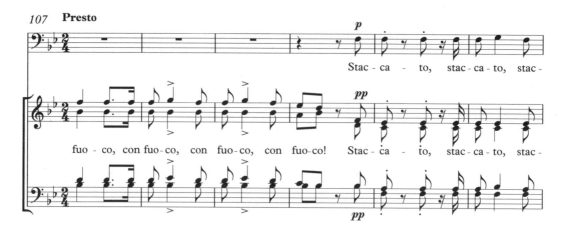

più la-men-to-so, as-sai scan-da-lo-so, non più la-men-to-so!

Recitativo

Bra-vo! Bra-vis-si-mo! So-no con-ten-to; Vol-ti su-bi-to l'ac-com-pag-na-men-to.

Schrimm! Schrimm!

Polacca con moto ($\quad$ = 132)

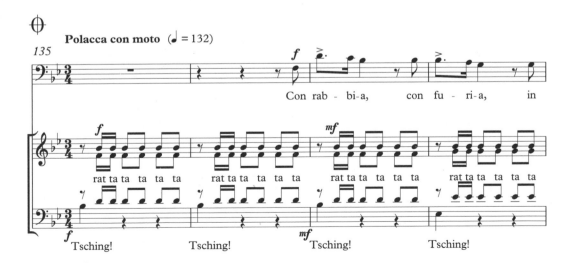

Con rab - bi-a, con fu - ri-a, in

rat ta ta ta ta ta   rat ta ta ta ta ta   rat ta ta ta ta ta   rat ta ta ta ta ta

Tsching!   Tsching!   Tsching!   Tsching!

11. Let's begin again

David Grant

JOHN RUTTER

This piece is from *The Reluctant Dragon*, an Entertainment originally written for the King's Singers and the City of London Sinfonia. Orchestral material (keyboards, percussion, strings) is available for hire from the publisher. Also available separately, x429 (excl. USA).

The fire-light in your eyes _____ and the can - dle-light

Ev-'ry crea - ture soft - ly bless, Touch-ing each with ten - der-ness, ____

Help-ing us to see, To see a bet-ter way a - head. ____

* Alto part optional

unis. **pp** *very gently*

4. The man-tle of the night _____ wraps things

pp *very gently*

8 _ _ _ _ _ _ _

dim. **pp** *molto legato*

Ped. * Ped. * Ped. *

si - lent-ly; _____ No-thing mor-tal shows; _____ Let's step

poco cresc.

poco cresc.

mp _____ *mf*

care - ful-ly; Make new tracks to - geth - er, Walk hand in

mp _____ *mf*

mp *cresc.* *mf*

12. Londonderry Air

Frederick Weatherly

Traditional Irish
arr.: BOB CHILCOTT

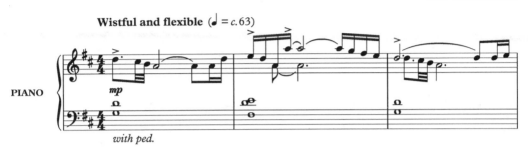

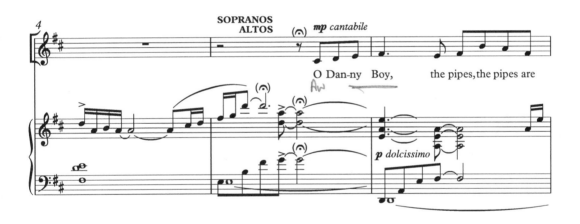

The accompaniment is scored for 2 flutes, 2 oboes, 2 clarinets, 2 bassoons, 2 horns, percussion, harp, and strings. Material is available on hire from the publisher's Hire Library.

gone and all the ro-ses fall - ing, 'Tis you, 'tis you must go and I must

bide. But come ye back when sum-mer's in the mea - dow, Or when the

val - ley's hushed and white with snow, 'Tis I'll be there in sun-shine or in

13. The Lost Chord

Adelaide Procter

SIR ARTHUR SULLIVAN
arr. PETER GRITTON

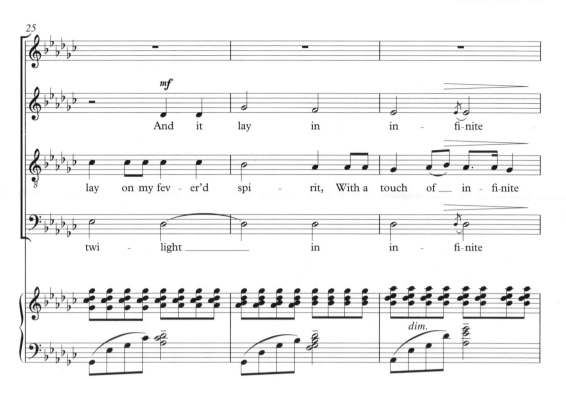

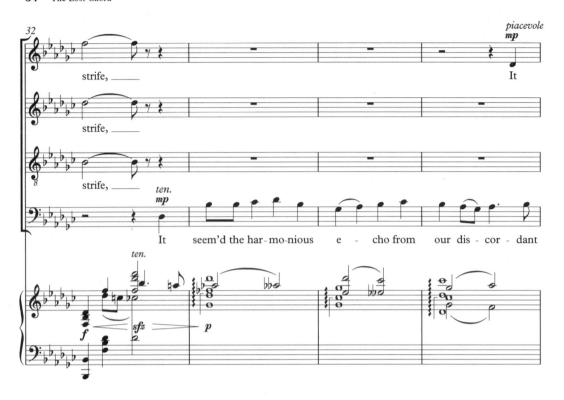

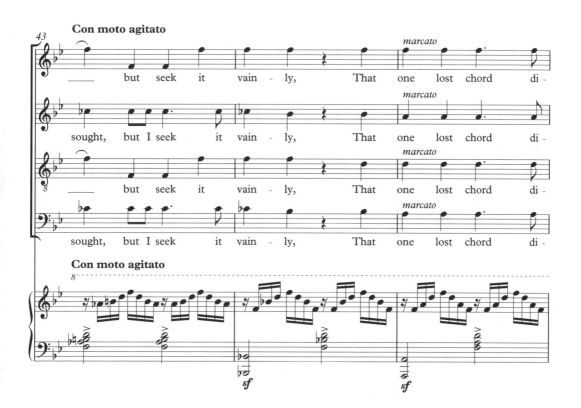

-vine,   Which came from the soul of the or-gan,   And en-ter'd in-to

-vine,   Which came from the soul of the or-gan,   And en-ter'd in-to

-vine,   Which came from the soul of the or-gan,   And en-ter'd in-to

-vine,   Which came from the soul of the or-gan,   And en-ter'd in-to

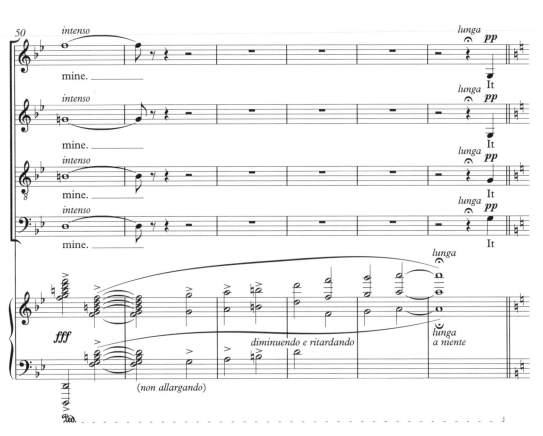

mine. _____   It

mine. _____   It

mine. _____   It

mine. _____   It

56 Tempo I

may be that Death's bright An - - - - - gel,

may be that Death's bright An - - - - - gel,

may be that Death's bright An - gel, Will speak in that chord a - gain; It

may be that Death's bright An - - - - - gel,

Tempo I

60

Will speak, will speak in that chord a - gain,

Will speak, will speak in that ___ chord a - gain, It

may be that on - ly in Heav'n I shall hear that ___ grand A - men.

Will speak, will speak in that chord a - gain,

meno **p**

pp

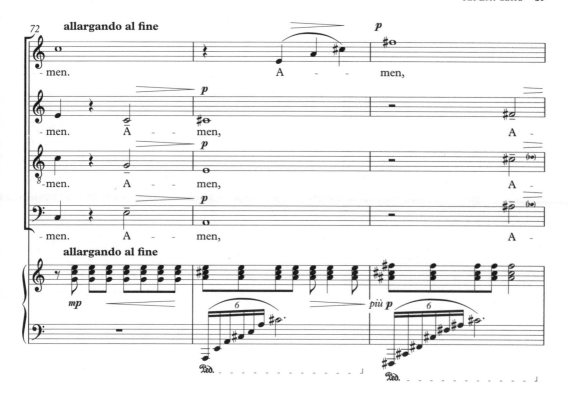

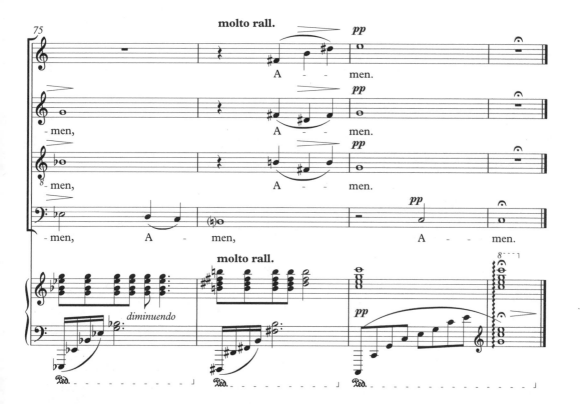

14. The Mermaid

A Ballad of The Sea

Traditional
arr. JOHN WHITWORTH

This arrangement was originally for male voices (A.T.B.B.). It can still be thus performed by transposition down one tone.

B. do not look for me, For I'm mar - ri - ed to a mer - ma - id at the

bot-tom of the deep blue sea.' 'Rule, Bri - tan-nia! Bri - tan - nia, rule the

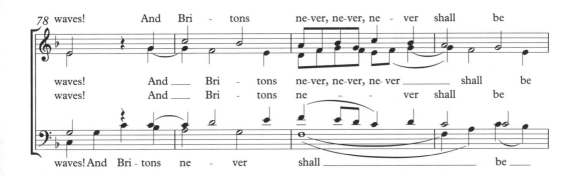

waves! And Bri - tons ne - ver shall _____ be ___

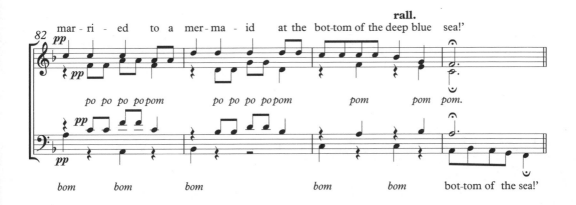

bom   bom   bom   bom   bom   bot-tom of the sea!'

(85)

In my chest you'll find my half-year's wage like-wise a lock of hair. This _

bom bom bom bom bom

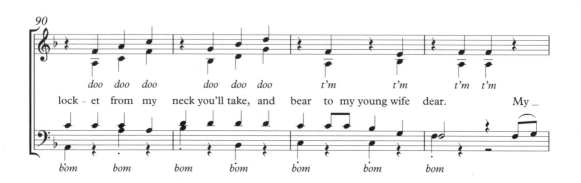

lock-et from my neck you'll take, and bear to my young wife dear. My _

bom bom bom bom bom bom bom

carte de vi-site to my grand-mo-ther take. Tell her not to weep for me, for I'm

bom bom bom bom bom

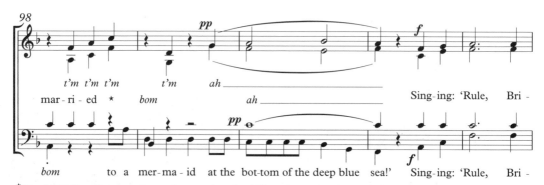

mar-ri-ed * *bom* to a mer-ma-id at the bot-tom of the deep blue sea!' Sing-ing: 'Rule, Bri -

bom

* For A.T.B.B. performance the two lowest voices should interchange parts between the asterisks.

- tan-nia! Bri-tan-nia, rule the waves! And Bri-tons ne-ver, ne-ver, ne-ver
- tan-nia! Bri-tan-nia, rule the waves! And Bri-tons ne-ver, ne-ver, ne-ver

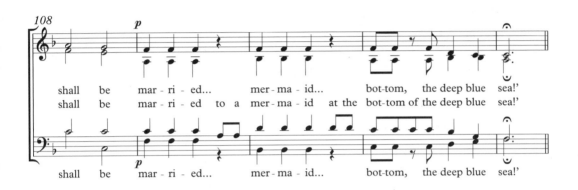

shall be mar-ri-ed... mer-ma-id... bot-tom, the deep blue sea!'
shall be mar-ri-ed to a mer-ma-id at the bot-tom of the deep blue sea!'
shall be mar-ri-ed... mer-ma-id... bot-tom, the deep blue sea!'

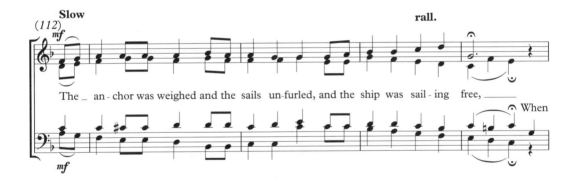

Slow **rall.**

The an-chor was weighed and the sails un-furled, and the ship was sail-ing free, ___ When

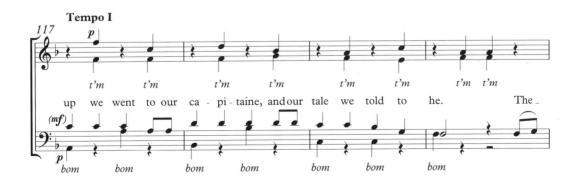

Tempo I

t'm t'm t'm t'm t'm t'm t'm t'm
up we went to our ca-pi-taine, and our tale we told to he. The
bom bom bom bom bom bom bom

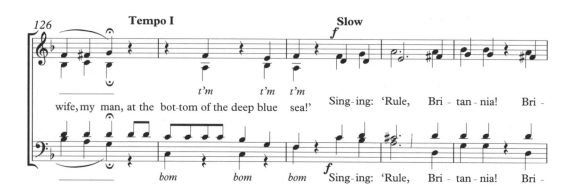

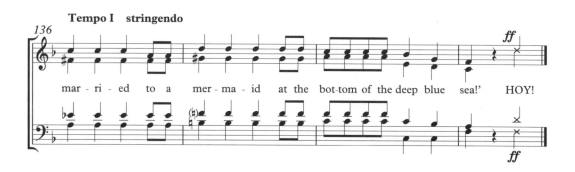

15. Name that tune

GRAYSTON IVES

Note: the vocal colours should imitate instrumental sounds as closely as possible.

* [Brass] = muffled boo boo boo, i.e. with mouth virtually closed.

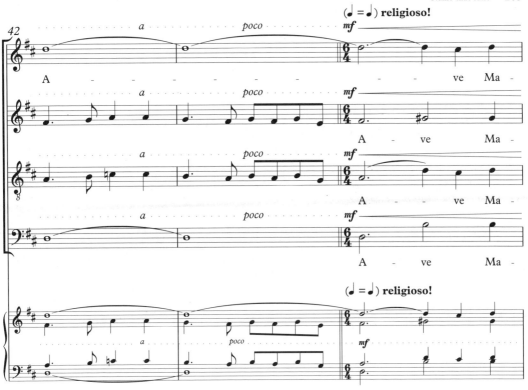

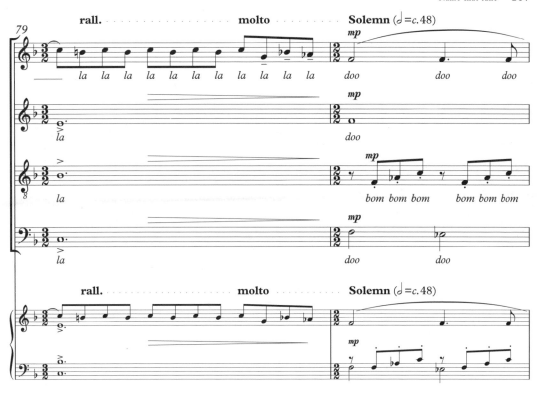

* taken by any member of the choir

16. Old McDonald had a farm

American Traditional
arr. GEORGE MITCHELL

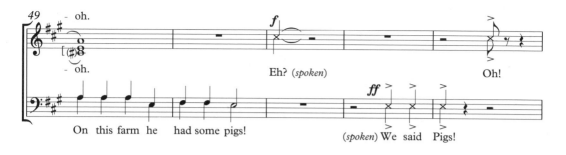

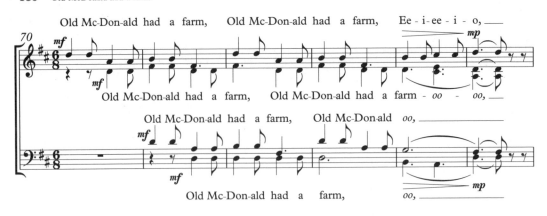

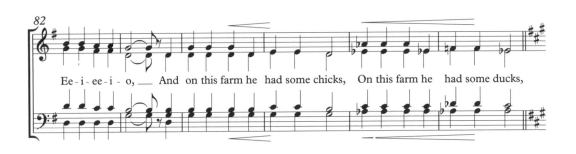

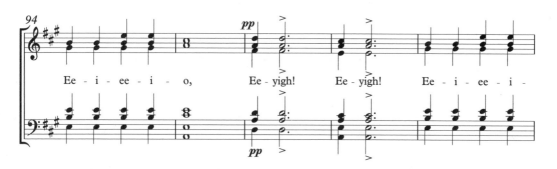

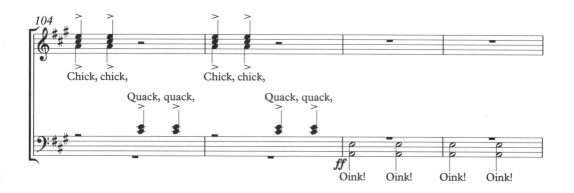

17. Quick! We have but a second

Irish Air
arr. CHARLES V. STANFORD

Thomas Moore

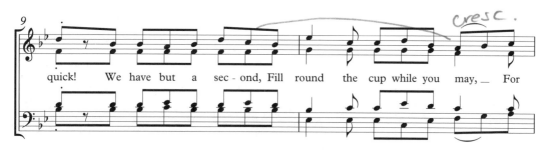

quick! We have but a sec-ond, Fill round the cup while you may, __ For

cresc.

Time, the churl, hath beck-on'd, And we must a-way, a - way!

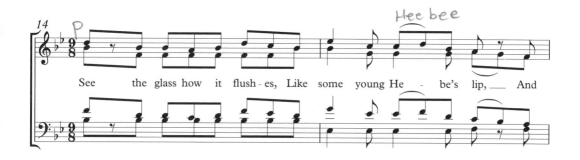

See the glass how it flush-es, Like some young He - be's lip, __ And

Hee bee

half meets thine, __ and blush-es That thou should de - lay __ to sip.

Shame, _____ Oh shame, If e'er thou see ___ that day ___ When a

Shame, Oh shame ___ un - to thee If e'er thou see ___ that day ___ When a

cup   or   lip, _____ And turn ___ un - touch'd ___ a - way. Then

cup   or   lip ___ shall woo thee, And turn ___ un - touch'd ___ a - way.

quick!   We have but   a   sec - ond, Fill round   the cup while you   may, ___ For

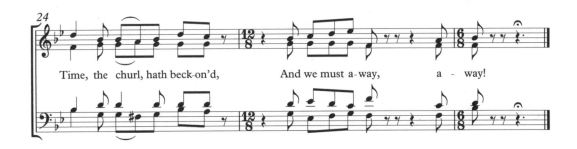

Time, the churl, hath beck-on'd,   And we must a-way,   a - way!

for Steve Race

18. Rejection

JOHN GARDNER

This song is from *Five Philanders* for mixed voices, commissioned for the 1975 Cork International Choral and Folk Dance Festival, at which it was sung by the Bulmershe Folk Choir under Norman Morris. The complete set is available on hire.

19. Sourwood mountain

Fiddle song from the Tennessee mountains
arr. JOHN RUTTER

* quasi double-bass pizzicato

This song may be performed as part of a set of three American folk-songs arranged by John Rutter, with 'Black Sheep' and 'Down by the riverside' (piano or orchestral accompaniment) as the final songs in the group.

© Oxford University Press 1976 and 1998

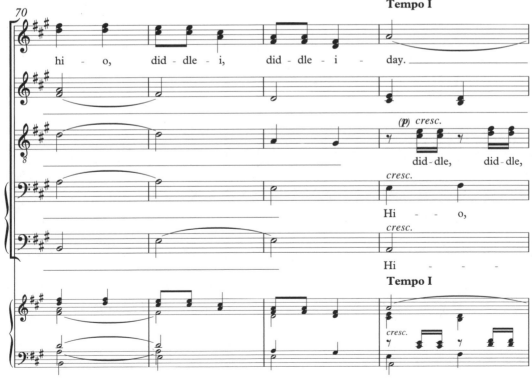

20. Steal away

American spiritual
arr. BOB CHILCOTT

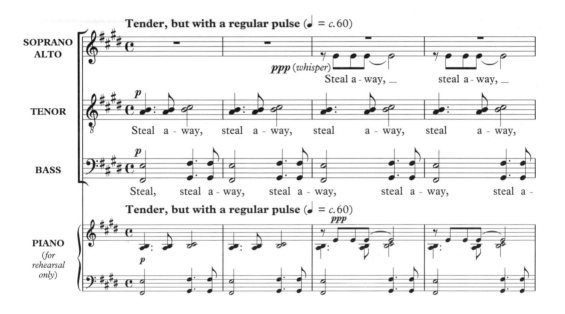

* top B optional

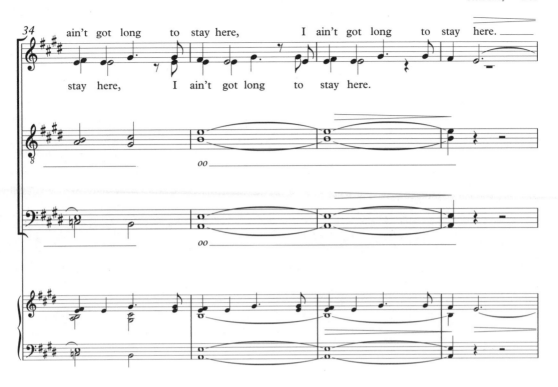

21. The Teddy Bears' Picnic

Jimmy Kennedy

JOHN BRATTON
arr. ANDREW CARTER

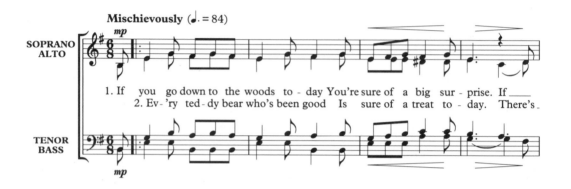

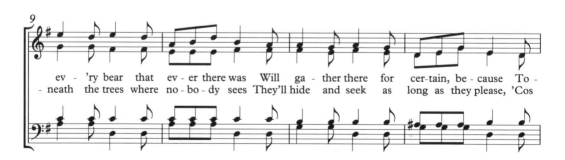

- day's the day the ted-dy bears have their pic - - nic. Oh, *every*
that's the way the ted-dy bears have their pic - - -nic. An

their pic - a - nic. Oh, -nic.

Pic - nic time for ted - dy bears, _____ The lit - tle ted - dy bears are
mp molto legato

Pic - nic time for ted - dy bears, *oo* _____

Pic - nic time for Ted, Have a ba - na - na, *oo* _____
f   *mp*

hav - ing a love - ly time to - day; _____ Watch them
mf

Watch them
mf

catch them un - a - wares _____ And see them pic - nic on their

catch them un - a - wares, *oo* _____

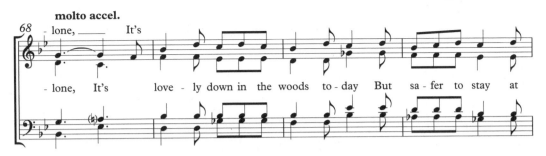

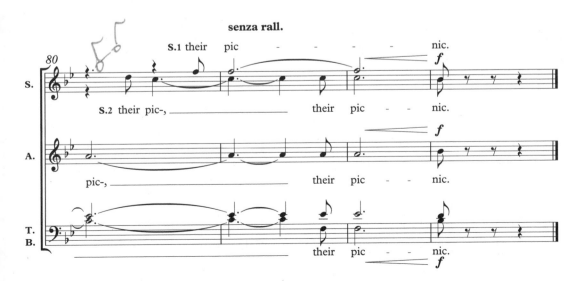

22. Tequila Samba

GUY TURNER

doo doo doo doo doo doo doo doo Te-qui-la, Te-

They call my love the girl who does the Te-qui-la Sam-ba:

-qui-la Sam-ba, doo doo doo doo doo doo doo doo Te-qui-la, Te-qui-la Sam-ba,

Ev-'ry night she dan-ces for all to see.

doo doo doo doo doo doo doo doo doo doo doo doo

When they start those play-ers play-ing, Os-tin-a-tos,

* Although best performed with piano, 'Tequila Samba' can be performed a cappella if no piano is available.
© Oxford University Press 1998

to my Mother and Father

23. Two for the price of one

A conflation of the two folk songs *There was an old man* and *This old man*

Traditional
arr. ANDREW CARTER

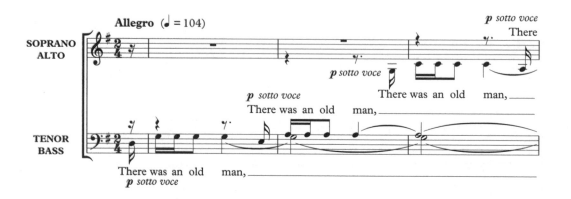

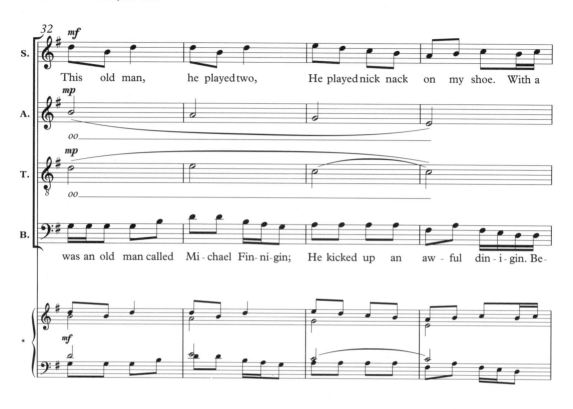

* piano for rehearsal only

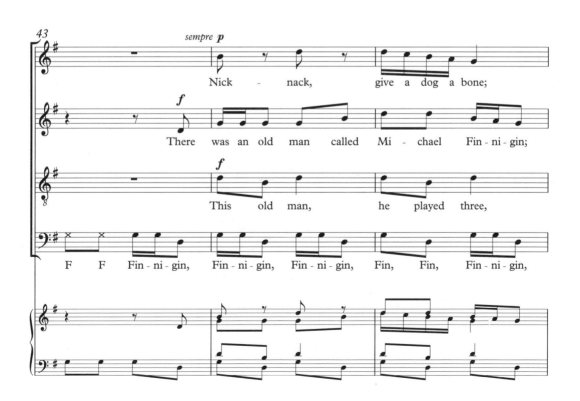

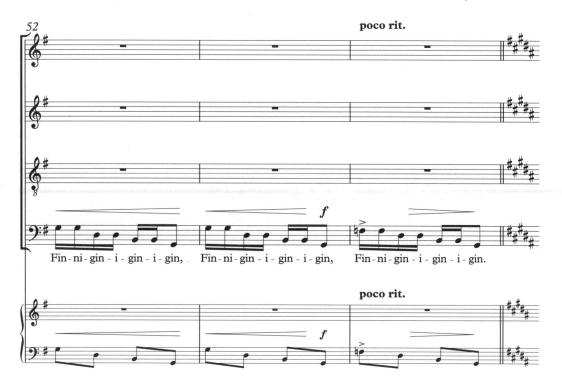

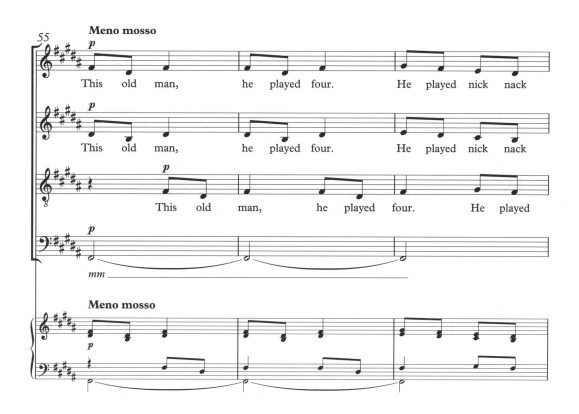

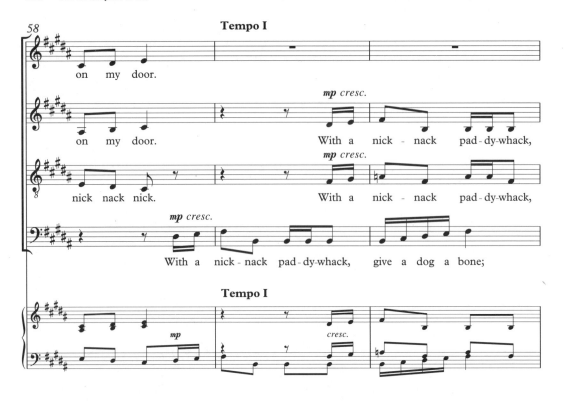

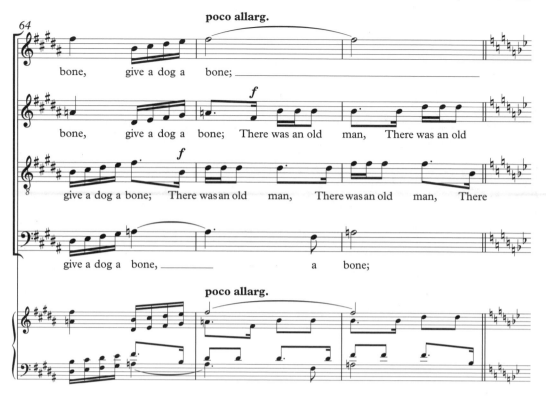

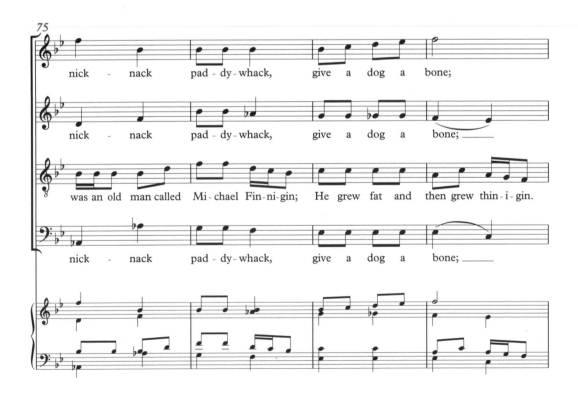

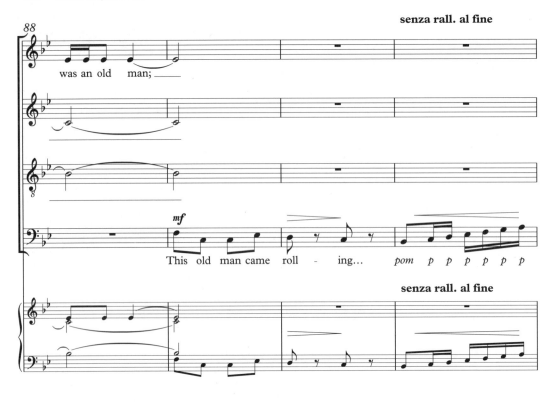

senza rall. al fine

Kurt Muthspiel gewidmet

24. Viva la musica

(op.43)

IVÁN ERÖD

mu - si - ca, ____ vi - va ____ la ____ mu - si - ca, vi -

vi - va la mu - si - ca, vi - va la mu - si - ca, ____ la mu - si - ca, vi -

va la mu - si - ca, vi - va la mu - si - ca, la mu - si - ca, la mu - si - ca,

va la mu - si - ca, vi - va la mu - si - ca, la mu - si - ca, la mu - si - ca,

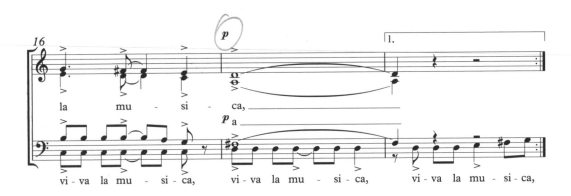

la mu - si - ca, _____

vi - va la mu - si - ca, vi - va la mu - si - ca, vi - va la mu - si - ca,

vi - va la mu - si - ca!

vi - va la mu - si - ca, vi - va la mu - si - ca!

* If sung by a quartet, omit the alto F♯.